Tiger

This edition published in 2009 by Odyssey Books, a division of the Ciletti Publishing Group, Inc. Printed in South Korea.

Library of Congress Cataloging-in-Publication data is on file with the publisher.

Send all inquiries to:
Odyssey Books
463 Main St. Suite 200
Longmont, Colorado 80501

ISBN 978-0-9768655-3-7

1 2 3 4 5 6 7 8 9 10 PAC 10 09 08

Tiger

Written by **Sherry Been**

Illustrated by **Cathy Morrison**

If you were a tiger,
we would call you **King**,
the biggest and strongest of all cats.

You are **powerful**.

You are **fast**.

You live on mountainsides,
in jungles, and forests.

You roam the grasses
of great open plains.

Tigers like to live alone.

Males make big open
areas their **habitat**,
or home.

This is where they
roam, hunt, play
and sleep.

Female tigers like
smaller habitats, where they
can feed and protect their
babies.

If you were a tiger,
we would call you
Great Swimmer.

You have strong
muscles and
you love
the water,
where you
cool off during
hot weather.

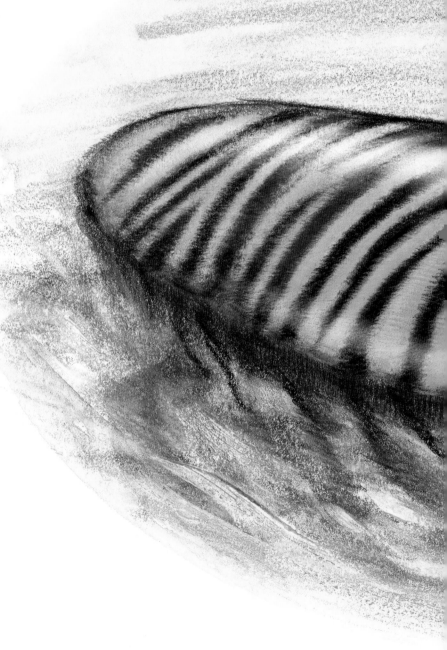

If you were a tiger, we could
see that your fur has **stripes**.

Your skin underneath
has them too.

Your stripes make
perfect **camouflage**.

The color and
pattern of your
fur make it
hard to see
you when
you are
among
tall grasses
or forest
plants.

If you were a tiger,
we would call you
Nocturnal.

You rest
and
sleep all day.

You hunt
and play at night.

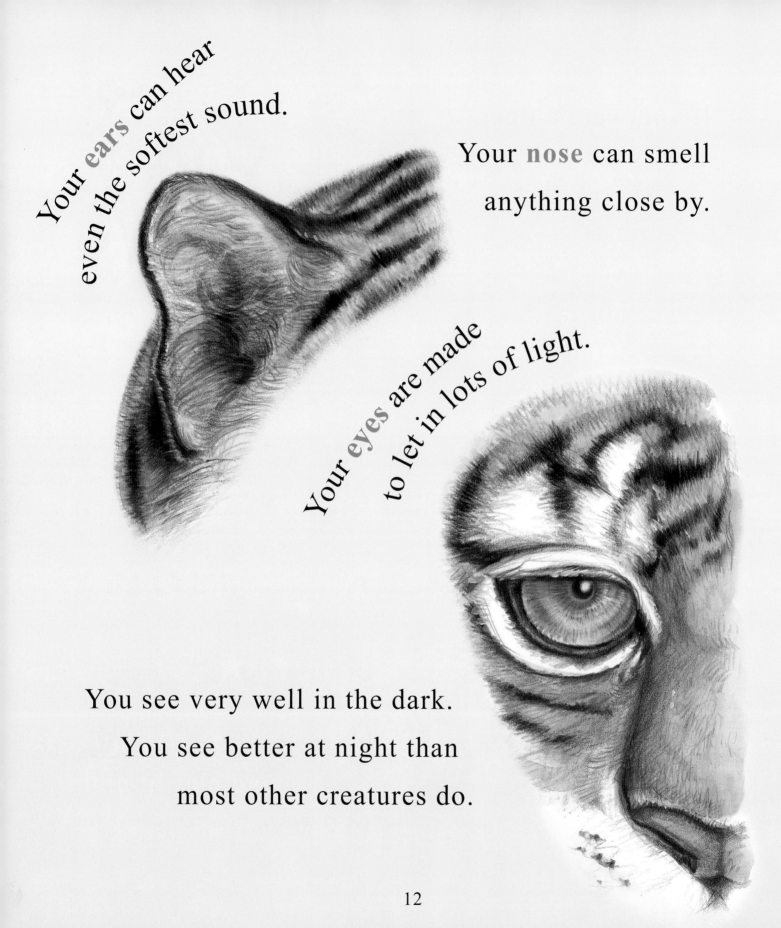

Your **ears** can hear even the softest sound.

Your **nose** can smell anything close by.

Your **eyes** are made to let in lots of light.

You see very well in the dark. You see better at night than most other creatures do.

Your very rough **tongue** is one of your finest features. This great big muscle lets you scrub meat off of bones and lap up water when you get thirsty.

When you **groom**, or lick your fur and whiskers clean, you cover yourself with your **scent**. It follows you everywhere.

If you were a tiger, we would call you Loner.

You mark your habitat as
you scratch the trees
and ground.

This tells other tigers
where your territory
begins and ends.

You do this every day
so that others know
where not to stray.

When you meet other tigers, you **chuff**
or snort when you want to be friends.

Your tail does some
talking, too.

Lowered and
flicking,
it says
BEWARE!

When it's up
and waving,
you are ready
to share.

You run on **toes**, which have very sharp claws.

They tuck into your foot and come out when you pull your **prey** to the ground.

Your front foot has five toes, and your back foot has four.

19

If you were a tiger,

We would call you Silent Hunter.

You silently slink and jump high in the air.

You **pounce**.

If you were a tiger,
we would call you **Carnivore**
because you like to eat meat.

Sometimes it takes a whole week for
you to find food, and by that time,
you are very hungry!

... So hungry
that you can eat
40 pounds of meat
at a meal.
You hunt cattle,
pigs, and deer,
baby elephants, rhinos,
mice, and even fish.

If you were a baby tiger, we would
call you **Cub**.

You are part of a **litter**, with brothers or sisters.

Your mother stays near the **den**
to feed and teach you.

Your father roams new territory.

When cubs
are born,
their
eyes
are
closed,
unable
to see.

After ten days, those eyes open up
and the cub takes its first look at the world.

Your mother protects you from dangers.

If she senses that you are not safe she
will carry you to a new den.

When you are a baby,
you get milk from
your mother.

Once you
start to grow,
she also brings meat for
you to eat until you learn how
to hunt for yourself.

If you were a tiger cub,
we would call you **Playful**.

You romp with your brothers and sisters.

You wrestle and roll.

You also pounce as you
learn to hunt.

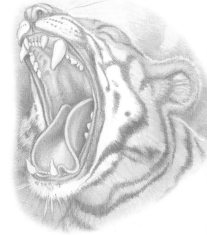

If you were a tiger,
we would call you **Survivor**.

You are smart.

You are strong.

You live long.

You are
King of the Cats.

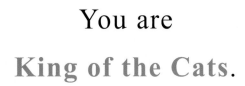

Tiger Talk

camouflage coloring that makes an animal hard to see in its surroundings

carnivore an organism that eats meat

chuff a sound like a purr that some tigers make when they breathe out

cub the young of certain carnivorous animals, such as the bear, wolf, lion, or tiger

den the sheltered home of a wild animal

groom how an animal cleans and brushes itself

habitat the kind of place where an animal lives

litter a group of baby animals born at the same time

nocturnal an animal that is active at night

prey an animal that another creature hunts or catches